WHEN MOM IS GONE

Dr. Katrina Boykin

©2018 Katrina Boykin. All Rights Reserved.
ISBN: 978-099164792-7

Published by Mattie's Seed Publishing, Greensboro, NC

All rights reserved. No part of this book may be reproduced or transmitted in any form or by any means, mechanical or electronic, including photocopying or recording or by any information storage and retrieval system, or transmitted by email without permission except in the case of brief quotations embodied in critical reviews or articles.

Cover Photo by: Adrienne Carter, aStyle Photography

Cover Design by: Iris P. Bryant and K&T Graphics

Edited by: Critique Editing Services, LLC

Dedication

To my family:

My deceased parents,

Graham and Lillie Mae Peele whose unconditional love, guidance and strength have been the wind beneath my wings

and to my siblings,

Linda, Larry, Debra, Janice and James whose unwavering support continues to propel me to my destiny. You will forever hold a special place in my heart.

In Remembrance Of

Graham Allen Peele

July 13, 1928 - June 28, 1973

and

Lillie Peele James

September 27, 1934 - March 10, 2017

and

Tammy Latrishia Boykin Raynor

June 11, 1963 - February 27, 2011

and

Mildred Kirby Boykin

March 5, 1927 - June 27, 2011

and all of my loved ones whose deaths marked out the beginning and the end of writing this book.

Acknowledgments

To God Be the Glory. It is a blessed privilege to share the wisdom that God has entrusted to me. I praise you, Lord.

I gratefully acknowledge the corporate effort of many people who were willing to submit their talent, experience and passion for a common goal.

To my publisher, Iris Bryant of Mattie's Seed Publishing, from our first conversation, you saw the potential of this work and have labored with me through this entire project to its completion. I appreciate you.

To Adrienne Carter, thank you for designing the graphics for my cover. It so perfectly speaks to the power of this process.

I am particularly indebted to my excellent editor and guide, Karen Rodgers in developing this manuscript.

To my friends, colleagues and my Baldwin Branch church family who have supported my vision of this book and the WMIG ministry, I could never name you all, but I am grateful for you.

To my husband, my love, Louie, thank you for your perpetual support, love and strong belief in me. With you on my side, I truly believe I can do anything. I love you very much.

And to our daughter, Whitney, thank you for always cheering me on. God's hands are on your life for something phenomenal in the Kingdom. It is for you that I do all that I do.

Table of Contents

Foreword 1

Introduction 3

Chapter One
Mom is Special 5

Chapter Two
So Mom Is Gone 11

Chapter Three
Living without Mom 17

Chapter Four
What Really Matters 22

Chapter Five
You Are Not Alone 26

About the Author 31

Foreword

When the words were penned, "If I Could Hear My Mother Pray Again…," that person must have been sharing my present feelings. A mother's love is irreplaceable, so when she is summoned by the death angel, and she succumbs, that is an incredibly painful experience. The author, Dr. Katrina Boykin, discloses very informative information designed to assist the reader on ways to cope with grief while living without mom, the chosen vessel. The death of any loved one is painful, but something about mom makes all things change. To be informed of the death of a mom is a challenging message to all family members whom she has served. The challenge and struggle of trying to adapt and survive can become overwhelming. Dr. Boykin without her mother is and has been the ultimate genesis of this book. What took you so long to invest time to help others is most appropriate because learning to balance the pain while walking in the will of God takes time. When *Mom Is Gone* releases the overwhelming feelings of loss that we all share with death. It will encourage you to live a strong healthy life.

When I was asked to review this work by Katrina Boykin, I was excited, knowing that her commitment to excellence in anything she approaches would yield an outstanding contribution to God's people.

I am assured that many will benefit from this work and be removed from grief and instantly begin to start the healing process.

Dr. Lillie Stokes
Clinton, North Carolina

Introduction

ONe Saturday afternoon while in Durham, North Carolina for a NCCU softball game, my husband received a telephone call that his baby sister had taken ill and was being air lifted to Chapel Hill Hospital. We frantically left the game to go to the hospital. He began to cry and slumped down in the driver seat of the truck. Immediately emotions began to go all over the place. Fear and trembling consumed our bodies. I grabbed the steering wheel as he struggled to get himself together. What had started out as a good day was suddenly overcome with, "Oh my goodness!" I began to pray to God for help. We did not know that this call would change our lives forever.

Doctors, nurses and what seemed like all of the medical staff was working hard to get her better. While we were praying and watching the clock, procedure after procedure was being performed. The look of fear on the faces of her brother and eldest son is something I will never forget. Hopelessly we stood over her bed waiting for her to come back. Finally around 10:00 p.m. the doctor came to the waiting room to report that they had run tests and tried several procedures, but her body was not responding. The final test would be done in the morning and that would determine her prognosis.

Have you ever experienced sleeping in the waiting room of a hospital? While surrounded by family, we all waited. Praying, crying, and trying to comfort one another. It was the longest night ever! Slowly daylight began to creep in. It was Sunday morning and only God knew what would happen next. The doctor arrived around 6:00 a.m. to tell us about the procedure and about how long it would take to do it. I can remember distinctly feeling sick, but I was trying so hard to pray and believe God. It was at that time that the doctor and nurse came in to talk with the family. He entered the waiting room and quietly spoke, "The last procedure that we performed on her did not work and I am sorry to say that she did not make it." Immediately wailing, screaming and shouting broke out across the room. This was such shocking and unexpected news until it was unbelievable. She was just with us yesterday and the next morning, she was gone. All of a sudden a quiet, childlike whisper filled the room. Her nine-year-old son began to ask, "Who is going to take care of me, who is going to read me my bedtime stories, who will help with my homework, who is going to buy me Christmas presents?" Sobbing with tears flooding from his eyes, he called out for his mother. She did not answer. Immediately our lives changed forever.

CHAPTER ONE

So Mom Is Gone

We can all agree that moms are special. After all if it wasn't for them, none of us would be here today. Women were designed and designated by God to bear children. That concept within itself makes all women special. Besides, can you even imagine a man being pregnant? God equipped women for an awesome task called mom. When you have a child, you automatically earn the title mother, mom, ma, and mama and sometime other names as well. A mother is a person who has mother instincts. If you stand in a room full of people and someone calls out mom, every mother will respond. Things you did not know or could not discern about other children now become so evident with your child. It's so easy for you to define what every cry means before your baby can tell you anything. A new mother will search all over creation for the right bottle, the right Pamper, the best crib, perfect formula, and the list goes on. What shall we name the child? As soon as the gender reveal party is over, the name search begins. No baby is perfect without the perfect name! A mother is one whose body comes equipped to carry a baby for nine months. Only a mom would be willing to gain weight, lose her body shape, endure weird cravings and endless pain to hold that special beautiful bundle of joy. When the baby arrives, everything changes. A moment of sacrifice for a lifetime of enjoyment. What a life changing experience!

Now the real work begins. Pampers, clothes, formula, teething, potty training, doctor appointments, terrible two's, daycare and finally school. Let's be reminded that parenting does not come with a handbook and sometimes it might get a little messy. However, growing up with mom seemingly makes everything better. Moms teach you so many things. When no one else understands or cares about you, mom is always there. Mom can make all of the hurt go away. She knows how to blow on and kiss every boo boo until the pain is gone. Moms will sacrifice and give their last for their children.

A good mother truly knows how to get the job done. In the midst of cooking, cleaning, working, washing and ironing clothes, she always knows what's going on. If you want to know how busy her life really is, just take a look at the outside of the kitchen refrigerator door. There you will find a calendar and a detailed to-do list of everything from doctor appointments to music lessons to football, track, band practice and the list goes on. How many hats does a mother wear? She earnestly wears just as many hats as it takes to get the job done. Depending on the circumstance, some mothers will work two and three jobs just to make sure their children have everything that they need. A mother will pray for you without ceasing and teach you how to pray. She will make sure that you learn of Jesus and know how He will make your life complete.

One of the reasons why life is so devastating when mom is gone is because generally a mother will stand by you until the end. She will fight for you and get you straight when you are wrong. A mom will give tough love and love on you at the same time. A mom, no matter how many children she has, always knows how to love each one just right. Plenty of times even in your grown adult life mom will come to your rescue. They will use their wisdom and knowledge to try to make everyone they encounter better. It is their assignment to instill values and morals in their children. It doesn't always feel the best, but it is always better for us. Most people today will tell you that they are who they are because of their mother.

Don't forget the grandchildren. Moms make the best grandmoms! They bake the cookies, let them jump on the bed when we couldn't, keep all the secrets, make every dance recital and sports event, send money to college and the list goes on. There is nothing too good for the grandchildren. Things that you could not get away with growing up somehow, the grandkids can get away with it. In their sight, the grandchildren can do no wrong. They love them, spoil them and send them home.

Mothers are the biggest cheerleaders in the world. They are always in your corner rooting for you. They love to have show-and-tell just so they can brag to their friends about how great their kids are. They will whip out the cell phone in a minute to share all of the pictures and put that proud peacock hat on too. A mother's face will illuminate the entire room as her heart pounds with pure joy when she speaks of the success of her children.

My mother was the baby of four girls. She grew up with a sick mom and a very strict father. Many of her days were spent trying to take care of her mom. She was a very smart lady. She loved school and was the valedictorian of her class. She prided herself on being able to memorize the longest part in all of the school plays which most often landed her the leading role. She played several instruments in the band and I can remember so vividly watching our hometown Christmas parade with her as a little girl and tears began to flow down her face. She was so overjoyed at how well the band was playing. She looked down at me and smiled and said, "Do you know how bad I want to march with that band?" Suddenly she started marching down the sidewalk with them and laughing. She made sure that we were introduced to the arts. She gave us her support in everything that we set out to do. I am sure there were days when she had no idea how it would all come together, but she never stopped trying.

She married my dad, Graham Peele and they had six children. Our home was always full of fun, food and laughter. My dad was a true comedian and he could make you laugh no matter how mad you were. Even when we would return home from church on Sunday and the pigs were out of the pen, and running in the front yard, he would make a joke. We knew that we had to go change our clothes and chase them back to the pen. It is so funny how when you are small you can't identify the struggles of life. In my eyes, life was great. My parents had a good way of making every day special, no matter what. Daddy worked hard, loved to make people laugh, loved to sing quartet music, loved his family and most of all, he loved Jesus.

Unfortunately after a history of being sick, he passed away when I was in middle school. I can so vividly remember the pain I felt when he died. There was no more laughter in the house for what seemed like such a long time. My baby brother and I were the only kids left at home with

Mom and some days she would look so sad. There were nights I could hear her crying, so I would lay in my bed and cry too. Losing my father really made me begin to take a different look at life. I could not understand why God would create somebody and then allow them to die. Even though I had older sisters and brothers, things were not quite the same. However, one thing is for sure, we will never forget how hard dad worked to build a strong foundation for the family. He had high hopes for us and he wanted us to be the best that we could. His many sacrifices will never be forgotten.

Mom took on the role of mom and dad and she worked very hard. She taught us how to work too. Even though she never said, I think she was worried that she would not be able to take care of us. She worked from sunup, to sundown. When we would go to the store I would never ask for anything because I did not want her to feel bad if she did not have enough money to buy it for me. However, in her resourceful way, she made sure that we were active and a part of any opportunities that became available. We took band, piano, baton, cheerleading and played sports. There was nothing like looking up in the stands to see her smiling face at every game or hearing her yell your name in the middle of the street at a Christmas parade. She was undoubtedly the happiest mom there!

We never went without, and with God and a fighting force on the inside, she raised all of us and some of the neighborhood children too. My older sisters and brothers were either in college, working or in the army. They welcomed every chance to help Mom out. When my baby brother and I became old enough, we both got jobs and tried to help out as much as we could also. Our lives changed a bit, but we stuck together and supported Mom. No one can take the place of your mother. You might not always see eye to eye, but one thing is for certain, a mom is special and you will miss her very much when she is gone. Never underestimate the treasure that you have in a mother's love.

CHAPTER TWO

So Mom Is Gone

On March 10, 2017 around 7:30 a.m. my mom passed away at Wake Medical Hospital in Raleigh, North Carolina. After a fourteen day stay in ICU, God decided to take her home. The most painful part of this at that time, outside of the fact that she had been suddenly hospitalized, was the fact that my baby brother's birthday and my husband's birthday which are on the same day, and my birthday and my daughter's birthday which are on the same day, all came and went with no response from Mom. The woman who birthed me into this world, named me and took care of me could not say a word. My biggest cheerleader ever! That smile and warm hug that I had witnessed for 56 years was now a memory.

She was not only the woman who birthed me, but she was the vessel God used to deliver one of my greatest miracles. When I was pregnant and in the delivery room with my daughter Whitney, the doctor examined me and found that she did not have legs. My mom was in another room of the hospital and when she received the news, she immediately began to pray, and the Lord delivered legs on my child instantaneously. God delivered! My child walks and runs and God confirmed that it was Mom's prayers that brought the deliverance. How could I just let her go? Who else could pray for me with such fervency?

I just knew she would come back on my birthday. I prayed so hard for her to just open her eyes, smile and say, "I know it is you and Whit tunes' birthday." But nothing happened. I guess I was just in denial and trying to pretend that this was not happening. Fourteen days of praying, believing, and trusting that God was going to come through. The doctors met with us every day at two o'clock sharp to give a medical update. The doctor's report always tried to shake our faith, but we prayed harder. We watched daily for one sign from God that she was healed. When her grandson came into the room, she gave her last response as tears rolled down her face. We knew that the bible says to be absent from the body is to be present with the Lord. We knew that she had made her peace with God and she had spent her life working to meet her Savior. However, we were not ready to let her go. There were too many things left unsaid. We just needed her to tell us what to do next. This is a memory that will never ever fade.

Hundreds and hundreds of people visited to show their love and respect for our family. No hour was too early, and no hour was too late. Often fighting back the pain and tears, we tried to greet every person with love and thankfulness. Soon we developed a system where all six children were responsible for a job and things began to come together. The hustle and bustle of receiving people, fixing plates, making and receiving calls, texts and emails was over. The task of picking out Mom's final clothes to leave this Earth and making sure she looked really pretty had been completed. Her gently curled hair was smoothly put into place and her make-up was breathtaking because she hardly ever wore any. So all of her girls stood in a stare trying to decide if it was too much and what would she want. Finally we decided, lighten the lipstick. When our eyes slowly looked down at her hands we all discovered at the same time that the nail polish had to come off because none of us could ever remember seeing her nails polished. So we all decided on gloves.

Our brothers and husbands quietly rested in the background, allowing us room to decide what was best for Mom while they struggled to be strong enough to get through the process. One look into their eyes and we could immediately feel the pain that was within the room. The unbelievable numbness of just going through the motions of doing what had to be done because no one else could, was beginning to creep in. We tried to continue on as if nothing had happened because realizing what had happened was just too unbelievable and painful to endure.

So, Mom is gone. Our family chain is broken, and nothing seems the same. The funeral is over and almost all of our family and friends have gone back home. The homegoing service was beautiful. It was exactly like what we thought Mom would have wanted. The music was a depiction of her life story. The church was packed full with her family and friends and adorned with beautiful yellow roses which were her favorite. It was a really different feeling because out of all of the funerals we had attended together in times past, today was her turn. She was lying there in her beautiful white suit that we had seen her wear so many times. She had a peaceful, yet still glow on her face. Her race was finally over and everything that she had hoped for was truly in Jesus.

So now what? An eighty-two-year-old vibrant and very smart woman named Lillie Mae who left home to get her hair shampooed and curled never made it back to us. Everyone was so overwhelmed and exhausted, but sleep was nowhere in sight. We were at the family home, the place where we shared so many memories of fun, laughter and celebrated holidays with good food and games, but something was missing. As soon as we looked around the room to find so many potted plants, greenery and flowers situated everywhere and tons and tons of cards, we quickly remembered that Mom was gone. How does life go on without her? She was the center of our lives. Everyone's day was surrounded by her needs. She loved on each of us differently and we all knew just how special that was. So now she just leaves. She'd spent fourteen days lying in a hospital bed while we fought with all of our being, telling God how we knew He could heal her.

It is something how scripture after scripture will come to mind, but the struggle is in your belief system. Do you really believe the report of the Lord? God hung, bled and died on the cross for our lives to be complete. The stripes on His body He bore for the healing of our bodies. Why not now, God? Why not now? I trembled in despair. My legs were so weak until I could hardly walk. My body felt like it had been taken over by aliens. I looked at my siblings and their faces all looked out in the distance. We spent most of our time just trying to pray and entertain each other. No one verbalized their thoughts often, but I could tell that everyone took their individual time to sneak away and cry and pray. Many family members and friends visited with us at the hospital. Their love and generosity were so amazing. Mom had given so much to so many people and we were literally getting it all back. The visits, prayers, cards, gifts, food, money, texts, calls all poured in daily.

We met so many people while living in the waiting room. People came in and went out continuously. We witnessed so many testimonies. We prayed and cried together and daily it seemed all of the families were getting good news, but us. Nevertheless, we had church on Sunday mornings and still continued to believe in an almighty God.

Mom seemed to be hanging on to God's unchanging hand. I wondered about her fight. She always had a fight in her to get it done. Was she finally tired of fighting? Something deep down inside of me said the moment that her sister passed away she was going to give up. Sure enough we buried her sister on a warm Thursday afternoon in March and Mom passed away the next day around 7:30 in the morning. The nurse said, "She just slept away." By the time my sister and I arrived back at the hospital, we found her lifeless body lying on a cold hospital bed with a slight smile on her face. Nothing had ever felt so unreal in my life. No time was allowed for her to say goodbye, give me a hug, to say how much she loved me or anything. She was gone.

So many times we discussed that one day she would no longer be here. She would often remind us when she was canning vegetables or doing something we did not know how to do. Gently she would say, "You better watch me because one day I will not be here to do this." Wow, what a statement! When mom is gone, everything changes. How many times in a day will I try to call or text her? How many times in a day will I say, "Boy I've got to tell Mother that!" I never imagined how many times in a day I would sit on the bed right before going to sleep and say, "Let me check on Mother right quick, only to then remember that Mom is gone!

Some say it has been over ten years and they still have these moments. I can remember driving down the road she lived on and thinking, I wonder what this will feel like when I am driving on this road going to Mother's and she is not there. Just a daily loud scream of her name seems to help me walk this thing out. If you are still enjoying life with your mom, then there is no way you can imagine what this truly feels like. My advice is to love and have fun with her just as much as you can.

Our last days together were spent on a beach trip to Myrtle Beach, South Carolina. We laughed and talked all the way there. We stopped to get food and we were still laughing. Little did I know that that was our last laugh together. Oh how I wish for that moment again! She loved me unconditionally until her last breath. My mom taught me everything except how to live without her. How do you learn to live with something that God has allowed?

CHAPTER THREE

Living without Mom

I have been trying to figure this out: Is having Mom die more painful than trying to live without her? The degree of how much it hurts is immeasurable. Reliving the fact that she is really dead seems to bring the pain back all over again. Forgetting that Mom is gone still happens anytime and anywhere and trying to control the emotions that surround that thought is almost impossible. Even though I know she is gone, it seems that sometimes in my subconscious, I forget. What about the moment you pick up the telephone to call or the moment you are on the way to her house, or the moment the family is planning a trip and we ask, "Who is Mother going to ride with?" Man, what a bummer. It just happened too fast. No matter how hard you try to move on with reality, it seems that living without Mom is such a hard pill to swallow. There are so many things that seem to remind you of her over and over again. I had the worst Walmart experience ever right after Mom passed. There were so many ladies shopping that reminded me of her, it even happened with the car that she drove. I was driving in the middle of the road and I saw a white car with a pretty little head sitting in the driver seat. It just tore me up. The different fragrances, certain people, church and civic functions, her favorite foods, her favorite chair at the table, her funny sayings, her favorite scripture and hymns. Moving on seems almost impossible. Allow Isaiah 61:3 to guard your soul. "To appoint unto them that mourn in Zion, to give unto them beauty for ashes, the oil of joy for mourning the garment of praise for the spirit of heaviness; that they might be called trees of righteousness, the planting of the Lord; that he might be glorified."

You see my mom was awesome! She left all of her children a cookbook of our favorite recipes. Absolutely no one can make chicken pastry, yams and German chocolate cake like her. She cooked breakfast every day of her life. We would wake up to bacon sizzling, eggs frying and the lid on the pot popping from the grits boiling. It was just like clockwork. She would be singing an old church hymn and going about her morning duties. I am sure she was asking God to order her steps while she ran the race. She made sure that we did not leave the house before making up our beds. She taught us so much daily. She did not teach me how to live without her, but she did prepare me to live a good life. She sacrificed so much for my foundation to be great. My mom would give until it hurt. She believed in lending a helping hand and she worked hard to convince everyone around her to do the same.

Most of all my mom loved God with every fiber of her being. She studied the bible and taught Sunday school for years. She worked so hard for her church that she loved dearly. She wanted to know everything about living right and her liberty that would come in heaven. We learned bible verses at an early age and quoted them each Sunday morning during children's hour. Mom was phenomenal. So how do you go on without her? Every day is a journey. But the bible says, "Take no thought for tomorrow because tomorrow will take care of itself" (Matthew 6:34).

Remember God is with you. Your mother would not want you to get stuck on the fact that she is no longer here and resolve to do nothing. No, quite the contrary. She would want you to make your mark on life. She would want you to remember what the bible says about death. She would want you to be positive and resourceful. Let the things that you have been taught resound. Nobody cares how much you know, until they know how much you care. Keep hope alive. Losing a loved one is devastating. Taking the time to mourn and grieve is very important. No one can put a time limit on that. So many emotions are still there. Some days you are just angry with God. You will know when you are ready to try to move on.

Remember you have to take care of yourself. Being healthy is one way to gradually move forward. Our bodies are our God-given temples. Trying to live up to the expectations of others will drain you. No one can know how you feel because everyone is different. Allowing stress to trigger unhealthy habits will distort your purpose and cause you to lose focus on why you are here. Seek help if you need to. Whatever it takes to get you back up and in the game, do it. You were created to do great things. God had a plan for your life before you were born. Amazing! He knew that there would be obstacles along the way. However, He did not come to destroy the world, but He came that the world through Him might be saved. If you give up now, then His plan will be alleviated, and the devil will win. Not so!

The Bible states in Revelation, We Win! You cannot give up!! This is the set time to say Mom paved the way for my success and now it is up to me to walk it out. This is God's plan for your life. He is your strength. When you are weak, lonely, and sad and want to quit, trust in the Lord. It certainly matters that Mom is gone to a lot of people. There is no control given to man over this situation. Truly it is a test of your faith, but you've got to go through to get through. Cry and scream when you want to. I promise you will feel better. Healing can be a lifelong process. The hope of God's future grace will sustain you in times of suffering. Those of us who are left behind have to develop strategies for survival. Navigate and implement activities to coach you along the way. Work to change your mind set about your situation. You are not in this alone and others are counting on you for so much.

Partner with friends who understand and can help you move forward. How will you continue on in life without Mom? How will you get up, dust yourself off, accept the will of God and continue to plan for your success that your mom has prayed to God for daily? How will you step up to the plate for your family, church family and the community? How will you make a difference in the lives of others? How will you help someone else live without their mom? What lessons can you share on this dark journey? These trials only come to make you stronger. What tools do you have to help generate and nourish motivation? Cultivate kindness while trying to build new relationships. Start a work-out program to foster better mental health. You can overcome depression, anxiety and stress by keeping yourself healthy. What really matters is that you remain physically fit and mentally astute to complete your assignment. So many others love you and are in need of your support. Now is the time to take a deep breath and learn to let go and let God.

I want you to repeat this prayer. God, thank you for bringing me to this place in my life. It has not been easy. Sometimes the pain has been too much to bear. My whole world seems lost without her. I just miss her so much. But, you said that you would wipe all of my tears away. Revelation 21:4 says, "…there shall be no more death, neither sorrow, nor crying, neither shall there be any more pain, for the former things are passed away." So today I give it all to you. Amen.

CHAPTER FOUR

What Really Matters

In the beginning God created the heavens and the earth. Then God said, "Let's make man in our image after our likeness: and let them have dominion over the fish of the sea, and over the birds of the air and over the cattle, and over all the earth, and over every creeping thing that creeps upon the earth." So God created man in his own image, in the image of God he created him; male and female he created them. And God blessed them, and God said to them, Be fruitful and multiply, and fill the earth and subdue it; and have dominion over the fish of the sea and over the birds of the air and over every living thing that moves upon the earth" (Genesis 1:26-28). And here we are.

God's creation is so amazing, and we were all created with a purpose in mind. While we were in our mothers' wombs, plans for our lives were being created. So what really matters? God gave His Son an awesome assignment. With you and me in mind, God sent His Son to die on the cross for our sins so that we would have a chance to choose life. Yet while we were sinners and His enemies, He had a plan for us. It is His desire that we have life and life more abundantly. In Ecclesiastes 7:1(b) (New American Standard Bible) it states, "And the day of one's death is better than the day of one's birth." This seems like a pretty strange concept. However, when we come to realize that a baby has to figure out the ways of this world and a death means leaving this Earth to go to heaven, it all seems to make sense.

Death is something that is promised to happen to everyone. Yet when it does appear we are never really ready emotionally, physically or mentally. It does not matter what the situation is that caused death to happen. Your loved one might have been suffering from a terminal illness, in an accident, criminally harmed and killed, unexpectedly or expectedly. Whatever the cause, it does not take the pain away. The bible in Job Chapter 14 Verses 1 and 2 states, "A man born of a woman is of a few days and full of trouble. He cometh forth like a flower, and is cut down, he fleeth also as a shadow, and continueth not." Verse 10 says, "But man dieth, and wasteth away; yea, man giveth up the ghost, and where is he?"

My husband, Dr. Louie Boykin, pastor at Baldwin Branch Missionary Baptist Church in Elizabethtown, North Carolina often states that we are all one telephone call away from having a bad day. Have you ever been going about your daily duties and your phone rings and it is someone on the other end delivering tragic news that someone has passed away? Suddenly everything begins to change. Death is so final, and God always has the last say. He wants us to have life and life more abundant while we are on this journey preparing to die. There is a lot of good to be done on this Earth. But, what really matters? Are we living a life so that we may join our loved ones in heaven one day? My mom taught me how to pray and trust in God. She talked about the love of Jesus to everyone. No matter what qualities your mom possessed, she had high hopes and dreams for her children. Will her living be in vain? If you are reading this book, there is still time to take the torch and allow her legacy to live on.

Ask yourself, "What really matters?" Evaluate your own life. Have you done anything to try to make a difference in this world? So many people are hurting and looking for help. If you were to die today, would anyone really care? Would anyone miss you or the good work that you did? Would anyone wish for you to be back here? Would the work that you have done truly speak for you? Do you have your final affairs in order so that your family can honor you with a proper and fitting funeral? Are you walking through this life, smelling the daises without a care in the world? Most importantly, did you take the time to accept Jesus as your Lord and Savior so that your soul can rest in heaven?

Sometimes we as humans spend a lot of time majoring in the minors and minoring in the majors. The things that should matter and are important, we pay little attention to, and the things that matter very little we spend all of our time on. The little things like someone did not speak to me today or my name was left off of the program, or someone cut in front of me in the traffic line. We talk about that for days. We get angry with family, fuss them out, stop speaking and never forgive them. Sometimes when a family member dies the entire family splits up over property and money. Feelings are hurt, and the family is left disconnected and dysfunctional. The family tree gets smaller and smaller, people are dying every day and you remain the same.

God speaks daily through his people, nature, signs and wonders and nothing seems to get your attention. If any of these things describe you, then today would be a good day for you to start fresh and start with Jesus in your life. What really matters is how we live while we are here on Earth. Live the good life that God intended for you to live. Remember the good times with mom. Treasure all of the things she taught you. There are so many precious memories, values, morals, and love that she left behind. Mom is gone and yes, you miss her terribly. She sacrificed everything so that you would be able to have the good life. Her living will not be in vain. Run this race with patience and finish strong. Endure until the end. It isn't so much how you start, it is how you finish. There may be speed bumps, detours and road closures along the way. Life might get a little tough, but God is truly with you and He understands. Don't stop! Get up and get going! Your life depends on it!

CHAPTER FIVE

You Are Not Alone

In the year of 2011 my husband and I unfortunately experienced the death of eight family members. His baby sister and mom died unexpectedly four months apart. While in the middle of life's work transition for him, we set out on a journey unforeseen. Making it on broken pieces was our faithful motto. We did not know how we would make it, but we knew that we would make it with the help of God. James 1:12 (New Living Translation) states, "God blesses those who patiently endure testing and temptation. Afterward they will receive the crown of life that God has promised to those who love Him."

Here we stood in a dark place, a pastor and a licensed counselor with no desire or ability to do either. There were so many unanswered questions and so many why's. It seemed so easy to simply have a pity party and give up. Everybody would understand that life's troubles had gotten the best of us. However, there was something within that just would not let us quit. We were living witnesses that the prayers of the righteous availeth much because we knew that prayer was how we gained our strength to make it. We learned how to lean and depend on Jesus for everything. Funeral after funeral and tear after tear yielded an underlying strength to press on. You never know how strong you are until being strong is the only choice that you have. I am sure we visited every stage of grief until we began to heal and grow together. It was helpful having someone to talk to who really understood our situation. Although sometimes it felt like such a lonely and gruesome process, we were often reminded that we were not alone.

In Jeremiah 29:11 (New International Version) it states, "For I know the plans that I have for you, declares the Lord, plans to prosper you and not to harm you, plans to give you hope and a future." Jesus promised that He would never leave nor forsake us, so we had to rely on His word. Days when we were seemingly at our lowest emotional state, God would send people who were struggling with similar issues and from the depths of our souls would come ministry and encouragement that we did not feel we had. Even though the struggle was real, we continued to fight the good fight of faith. We came to realize that families experience death and other life tragedies every day. No one is exempt.

Do you remember the story of Job in the Bible? Job was a wealthy man living in a land called Uz with his large family and extensive flocks. He was "blameless" and "upright," always careful to avoid doing evil. God allowed Satan to torment Job. Job lost his livestock, servants, and ten children. Job tore his clothes and shaved his head in mourning, but he still blessed God in his prayers. Then he was afflicted with horrible skin sores. His wife encouraged him to curse God and to give up and die, but Job refused. His friends even questioned him. Nevertheless, Job continued to trust in God. God gave Job more at the end than he had at the beginning. Should innocent persons have to suffer when the wicked escape suffering and are permitted to have comfort and security? Job never complained, he just kept believing.

This is a good message for all of us. Difficult times become a special invitation for us to grow. An old gospel hymn says each victory will help you, some other to win. You have to go through to get through. There truly is victory in Jesus. God knew the battle would be tough, but He wants us to cast our cares upon Him, because He cares for us. "Whatsoever things are true, whatsoever things are honest, whatsoever things are just, whatsoever things are pure, whatsoever things are lovely, whatsoever things are of a good report, if there be any virtue, and if there be any praise, think on these things" (Philippians 4:8). The joy of the Lord will prove to be your strength and if you keep your mind on Him, He will keep you in perfect peace.

It is my prayer today that you will heal from your loss and begin to get back to a purpose driven life. Rejoice in the Lord. No matter how bad it is, you can always find someone who is worse off than you. It is helpful to remember that you are not alone. Also know that God is able to work amazing good out of terrible pain. Remember, "The Lord is near to the broken-hearted, and saves the crushed in spirit" (Psalm 34:18 Easy Standard Version).

On September 27, 2017, my mom's birthday, I launched a new ministry to help families who experience the loss of their mom. I would like to share it with you. It is entitled, *When Mom Is Gone*. WMIG is a therapeutic, Christian-based support ministry that was birthed out of the pain of the death of my mom. This ministry has been therapy for me. I am thankful that God gave me this vision.

The mission of *When Mom Is Gone* is to

- Serve as a conduit to healing
- Educate on grief, mourning, coping, what to say and what not to say as we serve
- Aid families throughout the funeral process
- Locate services and resources for WMIG children
- Conduct monthly support meetings
- Provide individual and group counseling
- Provide scholarships to high school seniors whose moms have passed

This ministry is designed to meet monthly and work with families who are experiencing the death of their mother. We realize that the death of any loved one can be devastating, but the loss of mom truly changes lives. The ministry will track the families for the first year to offer assistance in any way needed.

It is our desire to get this ministry established in all churches and communities.

Please contact Dr. Katrina Boykin for more information using the information below:

119 Harmon Street

Clinton, NC 28328

(910) 990-7310

WMIG927@gmail.com

About the Author

First Lady Dr. Katrina P. Boykin accepted Christ as her personal Savior in March 1992. She loves God and his people. She has been involved in ministry for over 19 years. She is a licensed School Counselor and also holds a Doctorate Degree in Christian Counseling. Dr. Boykin is founder of Twirlers for Christ, a baton twirling, mentoring group designed for young and teenage girls. This ministry is founded off scripture from Phillipians4:13, *"I can do all things through Christ who strengthens me."* They twirl to the motto, "When they go low, we go high" from our former first lady of the Unites States, Michelle Obama.

After the passing of her mom in 2017, God allowed her to launch WMIG, *"When Mom Is Gone Ministry"*. This is a therapeutic Christian based support ministry designed to assist families with learning how to live without mom. It has been aired on local TV and it is open for establishment in churches and communities throughout the world. The Lillie P. James Scholarship, named in her mom's honor is now available to college seeking students whose mom has passed away.

She is married to Dr. Louie Boykin and the couple is blessed with one beautiful daughter, Whitney Nicole.

It is through her pain that she writes this book. It is her prayer that it will help others, because truly the struggle is real.

WHEN MOM IS GONE